# FENG SHUI *for* ENTREPRENEURS

## Harnessing the Power of Your Environment for Business Success

### Lynn M. Scheurell
Feng Shui Catalyst

---

**Feng Shui for Entrepreneurs:**
Harnessing the Power of Your Environment for Business Success
**FREE eBook**
This Book Includes a Free eBook You Can
Use RIGHT NOW to Upshift Your Feng Shui.
**Get It NOW at**
FlowingFengShui.com/Harmony

---

**MIZRAHI PRESS**

Feng Shui for Entrepreneurs:
Harnessing the Power of Your Environment for Business Success

Copyright ©2014-2020 Creative Catalyst, LLC

Manufactured in the United States of America

No part of this publication may be reproduced, stored in a retrieval system or transmitted in any form by any means, electronic or mechanical, photocopying, recording, scanning or otherwise except as permitted under Section 107 or 108 of the 1976 United States Copyright Act, without the prior written permission of the Publisher.

ISBN-13: 978-0-9801550-1-3 (paperback)

**Limit of Liability/Disclaimer of Warranty**

While the author has used their best efforts in preparing this report, they make no representation or warranties with respect to the accuracy or completeness of the contents and specifically disclaim any implied warranties. The advice and strategies contained herein may not be suitable for your situation. You should consult with a professional where appropriate. The author shall not be liable for any loss of profit or any other commercial damages, including but not limited to special, incidental, consequential or other damages.

Published by Mizrahi Press
A Division of Creative Catalyst LLC
**MyCreativeCatalyst.com**

*With gratitude and good energy for all
who have shared their Feng Shui
wisdom, experience and spaces with me.*

# Table of Contents

*Foreword*　vii

*Testimonials*　ix

*Introduction*　xi

Definition and Brief History of Feng Shui　1

Definition and Principles of Chi　5

Theory of Relativity　11

The Five Aspects of Destiny　13

Overview of The Five Nature Element Theory　15

Self-Assessment for Five Element Typing　21

Personality Qualities of the Five Elements　27

The Bagua Map　33

Symbolism and Adjustments　39

Entrepreneurial Essentials and Red Flags　49

Activating Your Environment　55

Your Feng Shui Action Plan　57

In Closing　61

Appendices　63

The Top Ten Ways That Feng Shui Supports You　65

The Feng Shui of Logos    71

Top Ten Reasons to Feng Shui Both Your Home and Office    73

Feng Shui Frequently Asked Questions    77

Glossary of Feng Shui Terms    81

Feng Shui Self-Quiz    85

Bonus    87

*About the Author*    89

*Other Books By Lynn Scheurell*    93

# Foreword

It is human nature to want new results with minimal effort. It is also human nature to forget the pain points when we celebrate those new results. To get the most out of your experience in working with your Feng Shui—meaning, to get the most robust awareness of your transformations—you must know your current state as well as what evolves next from making changes in your environment. By making an assessment of what IS before you begin, you will have more to celebrate when you achieve your goals.

Feng Shui is a highly personal process in that what works for someone else may not work for you. I learned this when I saw one of my clients beating his desk with a broom. It turned out he had a neighbor who worked with a Feng Shui practitioner who recommended beating the neighbor's desk with a broom to knock out the bad spirits of the desk. As my client had no negative energies around his desk, this 'cure' did not apply to him. (If anything, he was creating negative energy through a nonsensical violent motion.)

Also, Feng Shui is relative in that what works in one situation for you may not work in another, or to varying degrees. For example, activating your love life may not have any impact on the quality of clients or customers you are attracting through your business.

It is important you know these things in advance to have appropriate expectations about what it means to work with your Feng Shui. The process is a bit like decoding your personal recipe for your favorite food—except you are discovering your secret ingredients in the right ratios in a mixing process that is right for you with the right utensils and best timing as you create your culinary masterpiece.

May you gain new insights to grow your business faster and easier by intentionally working with your environment(s).

# Testimonials

What people are saying about Lynn Scheurell:

"Lynn performed a Feng Shui cleansing at my company on a Sunday, when there were no employees in the building. Without being told, she intuitively knew information about some of our employees. For example, she 'felt' a difficulty in breathing in one, cramped, shared office. One of the women who worked there had a lung transplant (and has since been moved to a private, airy office). At Lynn's suggestion, we hired a consultant who mentored all of our managers, including the C.E.O. As a result we have gained efficiency, productivity and increased sales. We've outgrown our former building and moved to a newer, larger facility where we continue to grow."

~ Julie Greenspan, Business Owner

"Lynn Scheurell has feng shuied my professional office, my husband's office and both of my children's bedrooms. As for the offices, I can't articulate how wonderful the energy is in both of them, and how transformed they became based on her work. Almost 100% of my clients comment on how good the space feels. As for my kids' rooms. My daughter had moved her bed against and blocking a door, and in the same time, her teenage life had fallen apart! Lynn had her shift several things, and what was broken became whole again. My son says many nights of the week when he's doing homework, "Don't you love the way my room feels?" This work is for real! Thank you Lynn!"

~ C.B., Psychotherapist

"Before Lynn Scheurell coached me, I dreamed and planned about being mentally free to do what I love – a successful coach and speaker. The fear of being incomprehensible blocked me from ever doing large workshops and conferences. Now that Lynn Scheurell is my Catalyst, I have her incredible energy combined with her Feng Shui talents which allows me to feel supported in all areas of my life. I have become so confident in my life purpose that I feel I am always at the right place, at the right time, doing the right thing. I finally feel alive, being my authentic self. It's as if I learned to walk for the first time. My journey has just begun. Thank you."

~ Rodney Sapini, Executive Coach


"I have always been fascinated with Feng Shui, but never understood how to implement it and figure out which corner was what or where in the spaces I had lived throughout my life. I recently moved into a brand new flat complex and was the first occupant for my flat. I asked Lynn to come through and Feng Shui this space properly as I wanted it to have the right flow especially since I was dealing with a blank slate.

Throughout the consultation, I was in awe at her vision and master skillset. She was pointing things out left, right and center. After fixing and adding some things to make the space softer, my flat had even a more peaceful feeling than when I first moved in.

Then we did a space clearing. I knew it would be a great idea but didn't realize the impact of it until we completed the clearing. The colors of my 6-year old furniture really popped! The lines of the flat softened even further, the light reflected brighter throughout the flat, my art work brightened with more vivid colors – even my foster dog became more relaxed and peaceful!

Leading up to the clearing, I had not been sleeping well at all; the night after the clearing, I had the best nights' sleep in I don't know how long! This effect spilled into my work too as I do a lot of work from home. I started feeling more creative. Prior to the clearing, my work had fits and starts; after the clearing, everything was flowing along. Now it seems as if there is no stopping – and I'm not complaining in the least!"

~ Shelley Kaplar, Vitality Optimizer

# Introduction

You are a leader in discovering business opportunities and, as a result, look for ways to optimize your investments of time, energy and resources. In Feng Shui, which is the practical harmonization of your environment with your intentions in right timing, it is said that your environment is the most significant path to creating success. Why? Because just like even the most vibrant fish cannot thrive in a dirty tank, your business cannot thrive in a negative environment.

By applying the power of Feng Shui to achieve a new relationship with your environments, you can program your business success. This book is designed to give you practical tools and techniques you can use immediately to enhance all that you create and experience through the conscious application of Feng Shui principles and practices.

As a result of this book, you will:

1. Create a personal Feng Shui Action Plan.

2. Develop a general understanding of Feng Shui, including floor plans and five element theory.

3. Know and apply the principles of energy.

4. Be able to informally assess the Feng Shui of any environment.

5. Explore personal Feng Shui personality and needs.

# Definition and Brief History of Feng Shui

*"Let us not look back in anger or forward in fear, but around in awareness."*

~ James Thurber

*F*eng Shui, pronounced *fung shway*, is a 4,000-year-old Chinese art and science based on understanding the blend of our personal energy and the vibrations of the energy in our surroundings—our external body—affect the balance we experience in life. This exchange of energy can work one of two ways: 1) be an inspiring influence to help us realize our goals, or 2) have an overwhelming effect, draining our resources and putting obstacles in our way.

By aligning your personal energy with your environment through placing physical elemental qualities colors and shapes in "auspicious" positions around you, you can positively influence your wealth, relationships, health and businesses. Naturally, you can either enhance or detract from your ability to achieve your business goals based on your environments.

As an example, consider what it would be like to have the most spectacular stove you could imagine—with extra features, more burners and gourmet-kitchen styling. Then place that fabulous stove in a house that's in shambles… nearly falling down… burned out…

with holes in the roof. It no longer matters how amazing that stove is because the house is not worthy and cannot support its brilliance. That is the power of Feng Shui in action. Unfortunately, many people do not realize that their house—their external body—is in disarray.

Every culture has a belief system about working with natural energy flow; Feng Shui has enjoyed 'fad' status as it has become more mainstream than others.

The words "feng" and "shui" literally mean "wind" and "water", which are the only two things humans cannot live without (for very long anyway!). The main objective of Feng Shui is for you to be in harmony with your life and goals at this time in your life and in your current environment(s). That is, there are four elements to positive and supportive personal Feng Shui: you, your goals, your environment, at this time. There are many schools of Feng Shui; this book is based on the tools and techniques of the Black Sect of Tantric Buddhism school (commonly known as "Black Hat" Feng Shui) as founded by Grand Master Lin Yun.

On a primal level, we orient to our place in the world through time and space, so when our environment is out of order, feels chaotic or doesn't "flow", it actually triggers our survival instincts for potential threats.

That is, without having order in your space, you may find that not only are you unable to function optimally but you will also look for and resonate with negative energy. You might find yourself only hearing about disasters on the news, friends who are having a rough time or you might have a string of bad days for yourself. When that perspective is so frequent that it starts to feel normal, you could find yourself seeing everything through that filter of negativity.

When you no longer recognize chaos or negativity as abnormal, you are resonant with it. And that's when it becomes difficult to create a positive from a place of negativity, to create systematic order from chaos or, in terms of business, to bring positive solutions forward for

# DEFINITION AND BRIEF HISTORY OF FENG SHUI

your customers. You will naturally seek and express energy that matches that of chaos and negativity.

Unfortunately, because humans filter out the familiar (so that we can drive a car down the street without braking at every little distraction), you will no longer see chaos and negativity for what it is because it's now familiar to you. However, just because you can't see it doesn't mean you don't feel their effects!

Your perspective is the lens of perception through which you interpret your life and by which you make decisions. Your perspective establishes and reinforces what you believe. When your perspective is tainted with chaos and negativity, you will naturally attune your energy to it. Think about the last time you got sick… the dishes probably stacked up… you probably didn't shower until you felt a bit better… you likely had a nest on the couch with blankets and pillows… you might have had cough syrup and aspirin handy… maybe empty bottles from water or light soda… the worse you felt, the less you cared about your environment. That's what it means when negativity and chaos is stronger than your awareness.

To experience Feng Shui right this moment, close your eyes and think of being in your childhood home. Then remember what it's like to be in your best friend's house. Then think about your office or workspace. How does each feel? And do you know which environment you are in by how it feels? Yes, of course—the smells, the temperature, your level of comfort, your cellular memory would all inform you of where you were in that virtual minute. That is the power of Feng Shui. Feng Shui is the feeling you get by being in a particular environment. And, when it is your environment, you can literally program it to support your business success.

# Definition and Principles of Chi

*"Life is a symbol to be lived."*
~ John Fire Lame Deer

You may have heard of Chi Gong as a Chinese meditative practice, which is based on Chi or Qi, depending on the spelling. Chi is a Chinese word that is translated to mean "cosmic breath". Feng Shui works with harnessing and harvesting chi, or energy, just like Hoover Dam generates electricity by harnessing and harvesting river energy and wind farms harness and harvest wind currents to create electrical power.

By having an understanding of some basic principles about energy, you can focus your efforts to systematically create more of what you want. While I am not a scientist, following are some generally accepted understandings about energy.

## Energy is a vibrational frequency

Quantum physics is proving even the smallest atoms and particles are in constant, relentless, dynamic motion. All matter is comprised of vibrational frequency so everything moves all the time; in turn, that motion creates a vibrational resonance with everything else that is also pulsing with life force energy. The vibrations which relate to each other stick together. Why? Because it's easier to conform to a similar frequency than try to convert dissimilar vibrations to harmonize at a different frequency.

Think of it like a friendship circle… it's easier to hang out with people similar to you than to convert people with completely different values and lifestyle to live in a way similar to you. The same holds true for your client base in that the people who hire you or buy your products are likely resonant in some way with your energy; that is, generally speaking, your customer community usually looks a lot like the person who looks back at you from your mirror in the morning.

Which leads us to the next understanding…

## Like energy attracts like energy

Or birds of a feather flock together. Or it takes one to know one—same thing. We've already touched on this point; let's take it further.

If, on a scale of 1–10, an energy frequency is vibrating at a level five, it will attract other five vibrational energies easily. It might attract some fours or sixes but it's just a lot more work to attract energies that are not similar or at least in the same range. Have you ever gotten a referral and wondered how the project went so sideways once you got into it? This answers that question. You may have resonated with your referral source, but they may vibrate at a different attraction frequency so their referrals to you will not be anywhere near your frequency.

To break it down in simple terms everyone can relate to… if you're having a bad hair day, you are more likely to spill your morning coffee, be late for an important meeting, get stuck in a subway or forget an important call because your energy dropped in response to your bad hair day. As a result, anything vibrating in your immediate environment at that same lower frequency is attracted to you that day.

So the secret is to keep your energy at a robust frequency for yourself, where you feel good, so you can attract similar vibrational energies in terms of client relationships. Essentially, that is how you attract better customers. That's really key because…

## Energy follows, or takes, the path of least resistance

Humans, and energy, are efficient. Why take the hard way when you can get the same result with less energy? Consider energy as water—if there are obstacles to face (rocks), avoid (walls), get around (branches) or climb over (hills), you will see water goes wherever there is least blockage for greatest flow. It takes the easy path, unless there is artificial and external pressure applied.

Your goal in business is to remove the friction, or potential blocks, between your customers and making a purchase decision around your products and services. Feng Shui can help you do that.

## Energy is literal

Energy takes things at face value. Think back to a time when you asked for something and got it later, even if you didn't recall asking for it originally. For example, one of my clients felt on the outside of his industry; he 'asked' that someday the people who marginalized his work would come to see his value and ask him to co-host an event. It took almost ten years but it finally happened! And when it did, he no longer felt the need to go through with the event—it was enough to be recognized. The energy to manifest that opportunity didn't ask if that relationship was worthy; instead, the intention was set and the energy moved to make it happen.

Thoughts generate energy in ways we cannot see with the naked eye. Energy does not have the capacity to stop and consider whether what you asked for is what you really want… your higher self may do that through intuitive insights and inklings, but energy does not question your directives and does not pay attention to time and space in the same way as humans. Things will happen, just not usually on the timetable we mere mortals think they should.

It is also important to understand you receive the sum total of what you ask for cumulatively. That means when you ask for abundance five minutes a day, then spend the rest of the day unconscious and operating from the vibration of lack, the majority of your vibration is going to experience lack. That lack is what will be replicated in your results. So five minutes of abundance with 23 hours and 55 minutes of lack does not tip the scales in favor of abundance.

## Energy is non-judgmental

Energy simply IS—no judgment, no question, no second thoughts. Energy does not ask if something is right or wrong—it just does its thing as energy. Energy does not ask if it should be released in an explosion, a song, or hurricane-force winds. Energy does not stop at a line painted on the road, at a sign that says 'stop' or just because your checkbook says zero.

Energy does what it is directed to do and takes the path of least resistance. In the absence of direction, energy will meander. If you do not clarify direction for energy in your business, energy will create a relationship with whatever is vibrating in resonance with you—with no judgement.

So, imagine you do not have the number of customers you want for your business. Do you see your business as winding up to take on new customers who need your products and services? Or do you see your business as stagnant, stuck with products and services and no customers? Your perspective interprets the energy you feel, which programs the dynamic in your environment. This is a simplistic, but powerful, example of a common situation that can make or break your business.

When you do not give energy direction, it aligns with whatever is vibrating in resonance to your energy field. Energy will default to the easy way for itself without judgment. And energy comes back to what you choose to experience by how you perceive and interpret the world around you. Your interpretation of the world is reflected in your Feng Shui.

As an example, a client had been successful in her coaching business—until she fell in love and moved out of state. She focused on her partner's business to the detriment of her own. Two years later, her relationship ended. She remained in the apartment they had shared, swimming in the energy of that broken relationship she had poured her power into and now felt depleted and helpless. She felt she couldn't afford to move which triggered feeling trapped in the past, until she reframed her apartment as a way to be thoroughly complete with the relationship by reclaiming her personal power within that environment.

By recognizing that her power lay in her ability to choose something different, she began her business recovery by connecting with former clients who could reflect her gifts and give testimonials and referrals. Within a month, she had updated her website; within four months, she started public speaking and had her first retainer client. Within a year, she had taken an expense-paid beach vacation, moved to a new condo and had several ideal clients on retainer. In this case, her Feng Shui was initially virtual—her website and relationships—which led to an upgrade in her physical Feng Shui with a larger, more appropriate, brighter space for living and working.

## Energy is dynamic

As previously shared, energy moves dynamically, and is busy being, well, energy. If energy isn't moving, something is stagnant at the very least and/or, in the most extreme case, dead.

Newton said that when energy is in motion, it will typically stay in motion. So when you are experiencing a lull in business, that lull can feel like it lasts forever. Then when the tide turns and you get an influx of business, you can extend that 'wave' of business in a number of ways—being enthusiastic and grateful, upgrading your physical space with the proceeds, hiring people to help meet the needs of your customers, doing more promotions, upselling to your new customers, etc. Either way, energy in motion will keep moving in that direction until you focus it to move in a different direction that takes less effort than where it's currently flowing.

When your checkbook is feeling thin is exactly when you need to shift your personal frequency to feel abundant. For example, when a group of business owners was asked how they would feel and what they would do when they experienced success, their answers were often things like, "I would take a day off", "I would feel relaxed", "I would play hooky and go to a movie", "I would stop looking at my bank account every ten minutes". Ironically, each of these things is doable even without an influx of business or spending any money. By feeling abundant in the now, you can change your frequency around business prosperity, which is attractive to experiencing more abundant energy.

By putting energy in motion through intention, then supporting that intention by anchoring it in your physical environment using Feng Shui principles and practices, you create fresh momentum for the results you want.

It is important to be aware of these general principles around energy, because this book is about shifting or upgrading the energy of business success coming to you by working with your environments. We will consider how energy and your environments interact soon.

# Theory of Relativity

*"We don't see things as they are, we see them as we are."*
~ Anais Nin

*B*ack to our environmental basics… a unique principle of Black Hat Feng Shui is the theory of relativity, which states that whatever is closest to you has the most significance. While this seems simple, consider the truth contained in this idea.

When you want to feel good, chances are you take the time to wear clothes you really like, work with your hair to have a good hair day and listen to your favorite music or read a favorite book. You are establishing a positive personal environment.

Use that principle to create an amazing day for yourself. Make sure your clothes reflect who you are today, that your hair is styled to express your personality and is current with today's fashion, that you listen to music you really enjoy or actually read the books on your shelf. If anything is outdated, isn't of interest to you anymore, or reflects something you don't resonate with anymore, get rid of it. Update your clothing. Wear rich colors. Choose new books or music. Look for your patterns in your space to see where you can upshift your experience using Feng Shui principles.

A commonly overlooked item of personal financial significance is your purse or wallet. If the place where you keep your money is frayed, overstuffed, disorganized or unattractive, you are not honoring your money. If you tend to throw your purse or wallet around when you get home, you are disrespecting your money. Never set your money on the floor—make sure you have a place that holds your money when it is not with you.

One last thing to consider in your environment is who you hang out with; remember, like energy attracts like energy. Your social and professional circles are environments for you as well. Are your friends all people you are proud to be associated with? Do your friends support you in your growth? Have you made the right connections actively, or are you nursing relationships you don't even know why you have anymore?

There really isn't any such a thing as "good" or "bad" Feng Shui; instead, it's about whether it serves you positively or not. If your environment includes people who are not supporting you, it is time to get in integrity with your relationships because they could be affecting your business results. Putting energy into anything that doesn't support who you are now with your goals will only increase what you don't want, because where you focus your attention determines what you grow. While it can be painful to come to that realization, it has to be a consideration if you are honest in your intention to manifest money and abundance in all ways.

Think of it this way—if you have a limited space, say a box or a shelf, and that box or shelf is filled with things you needed in the past but don't fit or get used now, there is no room to bring in new things.

The same theory is at work when it comes to achieving your business goals. If the space you have in your schedule, work or home is already filled, you have no room to welcome the new clients, money and abundance coming your way. If you are not flowing, you are stuck in holding on to what doesn't work anymore and possibly even in some kind of resistance to your expansion. However, when you are flowing, you are in a state of optimism, joy and open to receiving the positive energy coming to you.

# The Five Aspects of Destiny

人生五種命運

*"I have always believed, and I still believe, that whatever good or bad fortune may come our way we can always give it meaning and transform it into something of value."*
~ Hermann Hesse, Siddhartha

Traditional Feng Shui practitioners regard the physical environment as the first place you can affect the outcome of your life. According to Feng Shui tradition, there are five levels of energy that affect your life in the following order, each accounting for approximately 20% of the factors of life.

1. Fate / Destiny / Karma
2. Luck (Heaven / Earth / Man-Made) or Calculation of Fate
3. Environment / Feng Shui
4. Philanthropic Contribution / Good Works
5. Education

As you can see, there's not much you can really do to affect fate or luck, so the first place to influence your life is in your environment.

In fact, your environment is more important than what you give as a benefactor to someone else or what you learn through education.

# Overview of The Five Nature Element Theory

*"The choices you make as you create your own image can, if well chosen, transmit a very positive statement about you and what you think about yourself."*
~ Schuyler Morgan

Before the time of language (and the internet!), the ancient Chinese masters watched the ways of the earth and signs of the heavens to observe and monitor patterns of energy. Over time, they organized what they observed into patterns, which became archetypes, of natural energy and chi flow. This system is called the Five Nature Element Theory.

The five elements represent the entire cycle of change and are considered by some to be the secret to life. They serve as a model for all cycles of change, from season to taste to age to life experience. The five elements support / break down each other, depending on the relationship (whether creative or destructive). This system is the backbone of Chinese medicine, acupuncture, face reading, 9 star ki (astrology) and more.

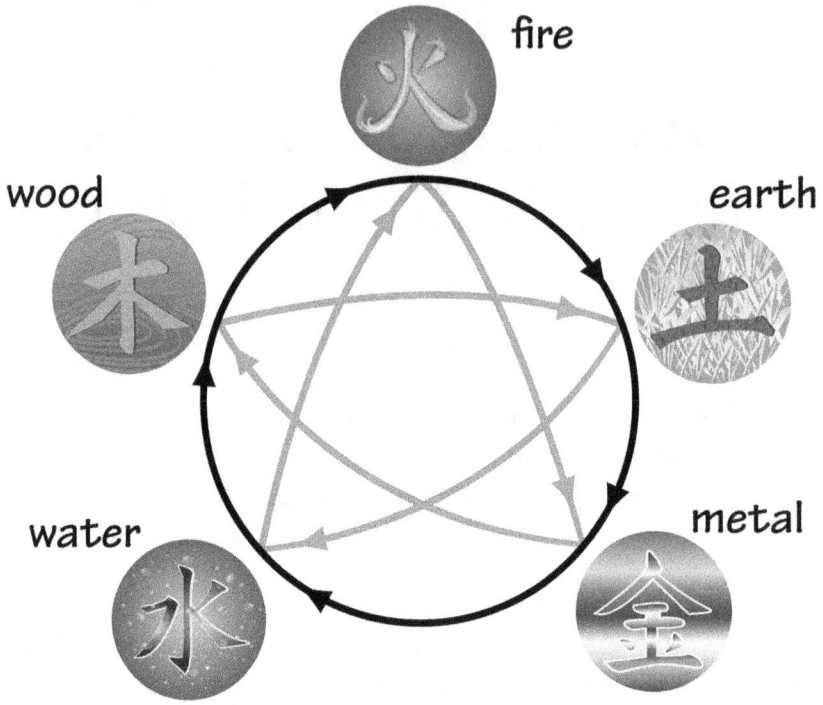

In Chinese, it's called Wu-Hsing, the Five Performers, and literally means "to go", indicating dynamic movement. The different cycles and "dance" of the five elements refers to how chi can flow, interact, grow, diminish and transform.

Everyone has a combination of all five elements in varying degrees. By understanding which natural element is predominant in your life and environment (which can be in different proportions, by the by), and how each of the elements present interacts with the others, reveals information about the goals you set, the risks you're willing to tolerate, the way you view the world, how you make decisions, the source of your fears, what motivates you and how you interact with other people (among a great many other things).

# OVERVIEW OF THE FIVE NATURE ELEMENT THEORY 17

Looking at how these patterns manifest in your life through your environment, personality, body and actions gives clues on how to identify and balance them (both excesses and deficits) to help each element fulfill their basic natural pattern in an intentional, conscious way. And when your personal chi and your environment's chi becomes unbalanced, it can have a tremendous affect in creating change (either positive or negative). The intention is to balance your chi with your environment for optimal harmony and support.

To sense the five elements as present in your environment, look around and notice the color, shape, or material any particular object is made from to determine its core element. Here is a quick list of how to determine the elements that are currently present in your space:

**Water:** the colors of black or dark blue, flow-y or terraced lines, downward motion, or the actual element (fountains, aquariums, etc.)

**Wood:** "forest" colors of green / brown, vertical columns, or the actual element

**Fire:** "hot" colors (red, orange, hot turquoise), pointy "flame-like" shapes, or the actual element

**Earth:** muted earth tones, squares / rectangles, or the actual element

**Metal:** metallic colors, round or half-round shapes, or the actual element

What do you do if you can see more than one element in a piece: look for what "pops" out at you most. For example, a floor lamp might be vertical (wood), with a torchier at the top (fire), painted black (water) and made of metal (so, metal). Whatever quality jumps out at you first determines the element (although some traditional practitioners may say only the actual element of construction makes that determination).

To balance your environment using the five elements, add a little or use less of a particular element to adjust for your personal chi AND your intended goal. For example, if you want to make more money, make sure you have water in your space (in Feng Shui, flowing water is flowing money). That said, according to the Bagua map, or energy map of your space, please use water in your Fire area very carefully! (See the next section in this book to learn more.)

Take a moment to consider your office. What is your sense of your office—is it relaxed? Does it promote action, feel energized, inspire creativity…? Is it comfortable and easy to work in with the right furniture and things you need to work easily accessible? Is your office organized? Each of these relates to one of the five nature elements. The list below gives you an idea of how each element interacts with the others, as well as the Feng Shui energy it represents.

## Water—Equalizing Energy

Water creates wood and breaks down fire.

> **Flow:** Flows from the highest location to the lowest, spreads outward, distributes itself evenly, provides balance, can be still or rushing
>
> **Colors:** black, deep blue
>
> **Time of day:** Midnight, stillness and depth
>
> **Design items:** fountains, aquariums, vases with water, bathtubs, pictures of seashores, shells and fish

## Wood—Creative Energy

Wood creates fire and breaks down earth.

> **Flow:** Disperses energy, spreads it throughout a space in order to infuse that space with a creative life force, roots growing down and breaking up the earth in order to generate life.
>
> **Colors:** green, blue
>
> **Time of day:** Early morning, the rising of the sun
>
> **Design items:** trees, plants, flowers, wooden objects like cooking utensils, tables, chairs, cabinets, cupboards, railings, paintings with symbols of upright movement, pillars

## Fire—Transformative Energy

Fire creates earth and breaks down metal.

> **Flow:** Expands outward, transforms energy patterns
>
> **Colors:** red, orange, "hot" colors
>
> **Time of day:** Midday sun, intense heat and brightness
>
> **Design items:** candles, incense, fireplace, lanterns, tea lights, outdoor lighting, spot lights, living things like animals, paintings or art with angular shapes

## Earth—Nurturing Energy

Earth creates metal and breaks down water.

> **Flow:** holds energy in and contains it to nurture and support growth, provides nutrients
>
> **Colors:** yellow, gold, brown
>
> **Time of day:** Settling energy of afternoon, things are ripening and maturing
>
> **Design items:** crystals, garden beds, terra cotta (both earth and fire), adobe or stucco, anything massive in size, statues, rocks

## Metal—Condensing Energy

Metal creates water and breaks down wood.

> **Flow:** Spirals inward, condenses and solidifies energy patterns
>
> **Colors:** white, silver, pink
>
> **Time of day:** Early evening, the glow of the sunset
>
> **Design items:** wind chimes, towel racks, tables, desks, hooks, mailbox, railings, shelves, accessories, bells, picture frames

The next section offers a self-assessment to help you discover your own five nature element balance as it is at this moment (yes, it can change over time). Be sure to note how the scoring works at the top, answer the questions, then total each section and list those numbers at the bottom. Once you've completed your assessment, you'll see the "answer" key and what you need to know about your own nature elements and Feng Shui needs.

# Self-Assessment for Five Element Typing

*A*nswer the questions with the following number indicators: +3 for most like me, +1 for somewhat like me, 0 for neutral, or –2 for not like me. Do not use any other number indicators (for example, +2 would not correlate to an accurate reading). After answering all questions, please total the corresponding totals for each letter; these totals are what we will work with in considering your Feng Shui needs.

It is typical of me (+1 or +3) or unlike me (0 or –2) to:

## A Section:

__ be cautious and sensible

__ enjoy frequent periods of solitude and introspection

__ be content being anonymous or on the periphery of social events

__ be considered self-absorbed

__ be involved in intellectual pursuits

__ be content figuring things out for myself

__ be careful about what I reveal to other people

__ be a stubborn defender of the truth as I see it

__ be patient and persevering in spite of defeats and dead ends

- __ be objective and dispassionate
- __ feel self-sufficient in or out of relationship
- __ choose privacy over intimacy, solitude over socializing
- __ enjoy projects that don't include other people
- __ detach from everyday affairs; instead, reflect inwardly about my life in the bigger picture.

__ A Section Total

## B Section:

- __ feel confident taking action
- __ feel powerful and invulnerable
- __ start new projects before I finish the previous one
- __ be comfortable with deadlines
- __ enjoy doing things that have never been done before
- __ act with confidence / assurance regardless of what others may think or feel
- __ make quick decisions and change my mind often
- __ be comfortable with tasks that demand "thinking on my feet"
- __ be direct or provocative even if it causes discomfort / embarrassment to others
- __ take pleasure in public recognition and admiration of my talents / achievements
- __ be comfortable leading or directing others

# SELF-ASSESSMENT FOR FIVE ELEMENT TYPING

___ follow my own hunches about what is right or wrong

___ to take the lead when it is necessary to get things done quickly and effectively

___ feel comfortable guiding others and directing their efforts

___ disregard other people's appraisals of me

___ B Section Total

## C Section:

___ be animated and enthusiastic

___ enjoy the pleasures of my senses

___ easily know what another thinks and feels

___ be comfortable in a very stimulating environment

___ openly share my inner most feelings and desires

___ live in the here and now and not worry about the future or the past

___ see the humorous side of life

___ be tender, intimate, and vulnerable with another person

___ be comfortable receiving and showing affection and pleasure

___ enjoy being moved emotionally

___ interpret life's experiences through my emotional response to events

___ easily become completely involved in the events going on around me

___ become deeply identified with the feelings, thoughts, and experiences of another

___ remain optimistic and hopeful in spite of what others may believe

___ C Section Total

## D Section:

___ be nurturing and supportive

___ put the needs of others before my own

___ take pains to preserve long term relationships

___ enjoy being relied upon for reassurance and help

___ enjoy being the hub of my social and family network

___ be agreeable and accommodating

___ help people work together in a harmonious manner

___ get involved in other people's lives

___ enjoy maintaining many diverse, even conflicting, relationships

___ be diplomatic and tactful

___ rely on the skill and intelligence of others

___ accept other people's characterizations of who I am

___ sympathize with the circumstances of other people

___ get close enough to need another person

___ D Section Total

## E Section:

__ maintain a neat and orderly personal lifestyle

__ be in control of my environment and the way I do things

__ be strongly committed to my moral principles and standards of conduct

__ feel secure / confident in my work when people are following proper procedures

__ enjoy tasks that require systematic approaches to problem solving

__ appreciate being thought of as meticulous and discriminating

__ be self-contained and not overly involved in other people's affairs

__ be appreciated or admired for my skill and expertise rather than my personality or emotional enthusiasm

__ accept the authority of those with more competence

__ be systematic and methodical in my work

__ be content with few close attachments or demanding relationships

__ put virtue and principles above pleasure and fulfillment

__ restrain myself in expressing my feelings or opinions

__ be tasteful and discriminating

__ E Section Total

## Totals for Each / All Categories:

____ A

____ B

____ C

____ D

____ E

## The Answer Key for the Self-Assessment:

A = water

B = wood

C = fire

D = earth

E = fire

The higher the number, the more predominant the element is for you, and the more the Feng Shui needs associated with that element are present in your environment, the more supported you will feel.

Following is a listing of the personality qualities of the five nature elements.

# Personality Qualities of the Five Elements

*"Surrounding yourself with energy generators is the highest form of self-respect."*
~ Stuart R. Levine

Each of the five elements has corresponding personality qualities. Following is a short list of those qualities. As you read them, think about who you know who fits each elemental archetype.

> **Water:** flows, fluid, adaptable, quiet, depth, yield to conditions/go with the flow, insight, philosopher
>
> **Wood:** vertical, growth, action, change, novelty, innovation, doer, pioneer
>
> **Fire:** unpredictable, expansive, scattered, passionate, intimacy, transformation, sensual, social butterfly, artist
>
> **Earth:** grounding, agreement, stability, permanence, supports, commonality, solidarity, balance, harmony, nurturer
>
> **Metal:** clarity, condenses, order, focus, precision, rules, structure, mental / intellectual, shine, aspire, problem solver

Remember you will have aspects of each of these characteristics and, over time, they may change completely. So, for example, if you used to be very flexible but now find yourself needing to be more organized, in the most simplistic terms, you are invoking your Metal energy to help you with systems and being organized.

## The Feng Shui Balance and Needs for Each Element

Each element is motivated by its own desires, and has its own Feng Shui needs. Also, if your highest number is really quite different than the rest of your numbers, you may want to look at the excessive traits of that element to see how it could be affecting you; likewise, for the lowest number, please refer to the deficit of that particular element. In either case, know you can adjust your physical environment to create a better balance, if that is what you want.

### Water:

**Motivated** by Quiet Time, Depth, Insight

**Supports** wood by restoring primal energies through quiet and solitude

**Drains** fire as caution and isolation defeat the desire to express one's self openly

Is supported by metal because systems are in place to allow down time

**Excessive water** traits are being afraid to take action or make decisions, being a loner (think rushing water—things moving too fast)

**Deficient water** manifests by not taking time to integrate experiences into knowingness, not wanting to be alone, hard to sit still or assimilate new things

**Feng Shui needs** are a meditation room, reading room or library, spa/hot tub, bookshelves, large CD collections, own computer, garden area

**Celebrity Examples:** Helena Bonham Carter, Jimmy Carter, Anne Frank, Woody Allen, Richard Nixon

## Wood:

**Motivated** by Growth, Innovation, Novelty, Change, Doing

**Supports:** Fire by generating energy to fire to reach expression.

**Drains:** Earth because too much action makes things unstable and creates dissonance.

**Excessive wood** traits are anger, volatile emotions, can't stop even if want to, starting a lot of projects without completion.

**Deficient wood** manifests as not asserting self or taking action, want to be told what to do, not finishing projects.

**Feng Shui needs** are to change décor frequently, open spaces, thriving plants, stable upright forces, high ceilings

**Celebrity Examples:** Tom Hanks, Linda Hamilton, Mother Teresa, Michael Jordan, Hillary Clinton, Kobe Bryant

## Fire:

**Motivated** by Passion, Sensual Pleasures, Sociality, Engagement

**Supports:** Earth by allowing the release of energy so that things can settle.

**Drains:** Metal because outward moving, individualistic energy doesn't allow for focus or obedience.

**Excessive fire** traits are to crave intimacy, staying superficial, lack of focus, being scattered, lacking personal boundaries

**Deficient fire** manifests feeling cold, being shy, being dull, unable to express, lack of creativity

**Feng Shui needs** are lots of light, open spaces, great rooms, large kitchens, fireplace in the bedroom, stained glass windows

**Celebrity Examples:** Meg Ryan, Cameron Diaz, Cyndi Lauper

## Earth:

**Motivated** by Togetherness, Agreement, Commonality, Permanence, Balance

**Supports:** Metal by drawing energy back to center after the expansive expression of fire.

**Drains:** Water because catering to everyone's needs muddies issues and limits individuation.

**Excessive earth** traits are feeling stuck, disliking or avoiding change, smother others.

**Deficient earth** manifests as lack of tact in conversation or action, unable to connect or empathize with others, flighty, selfish.

**Feng Shui needs** are soft, comfortable furnishings, dark muddy colors or earth tones, subdued lighting, table in the kitchen, farmhouse.

**Celebrity Examples:** Oprah Winfrey, Rosie O'Donnell, Eleanor Roosevelt, Julia Child

## Metal:

**Motivated** by Order, Focus, Rules, Precision, Structure.

**Supports** Water by providing the focus and concentration that precedes deep thinking.

**Drains** Wood as too much attention to rules blocks and inhibits creation and innovation (metal chops wood).

**Excessive metal** traits are rigid thinking, rule bound, unable to think outside the box.

**Deficient metal** manifests as feeling invulnerable, above the rules, hates authority, can't focus.

**Feng Shui needs** are spartan and organized with modern or Zen décor, places for storing and categorizing, adequate cupboards, chrome or brushed metal kitchen appliances.

**Celebrity Examples:** Audrey Hepburn, Barbara Streisand, Fred Astaire

# The Bagua Map

*"Happiness is the consequence of personal effort. You fight for it, strive for it, insist upon it, and sometimes even travel around the world looking or it. You have to participate relentlessly in the manifestations of your own blessings."*
~ Elizabeth Gilbert

Back to our tour of your space… beginning thousands of years ago, the ancient Chinese masters watched, monitored and documented how energy flows through environments, from which they created a map of this energy flow. This is called a "Bagua Map" and looks like an aerial tic-tac-toe that is superimposed over your home/office. Imagine flying a drone over your house; the front door is always positioned at the bottom of this chart in either Ken, Kan or Chien.

Each gua (or sector) of the Bagua relates to one of the eight trigrams of the I Ching. The center area, or Tai Chi, represents the balancing force that brings all eight trigrams together in a harmonious way. This map contains the Chinese names for each trigram, the English translation according to the Wilhelm Barnes edition, properties, the element, season, time of day, color, and any relevant animals.

In "reading" your floor plan, it is important to look for major messages and themes of how your space is laid out and how that impacts your life. The next step is to consider ways to adjust your space for enhanced flow.

Some of the messages you get will likely be intuitive, although you have direct input into their meaning and how you choose to interpret them. The idea is to evaluate your environment for balance, major furniture placements, and overall "flow" according to the ancient Chinese energy map.

It is important to understand your intentions for what you want in your life so you can work with your space, especially when activating your environment with recommended items or actions.

One of my clients decided to make a vision map about what she wanted to experience—finding love with a doctor was one of her dreams. Her dream board had a picture of Dr. McDreamy from Grey's Anatomy, along with a picture of a Tiffany heart necklace (a silver silhouette with an empty interior). She manifested a physician friend who came to rely on her for everything from watching his kids and walking his dog to answering the phones in his practice to having keys to his house and access to his checkbook and giving neck rubs on request. When she finally got bold enough to ask how to move the relationship to the next level, she got a playful punch on the arm and said, 'we're just good buddies, aren't we?' So she got what she asked for—an attractive and eligible doctor who treated her like a partner to the point where others thought they were married but where there was no real love in the relationship.

Working with the energy moving through your space is a powerful way to connect with universal energies. Understanding your floor plan and the chi flow through it is part of a dynamic process that has been used for thousands of years with success and can enhance the quality of your life.

When shifting your floor plan—and therefore, life—flow, acknowledge what changes occur, including noticing synchronicities, different ways of feeling, and new opportunities. Your environment can support you in creating the life you want—listen to your intuition, make appropriate choices, take inspired action, pay attention and honor the energy of your successes.

## Clutter

The word "clutter" comes from an English word that means "to coagulate". Clutter represents the stagnation of energy, a slowing of movement and a struggle toward making progress. As already mentioned, most people are more comfortable when the environment is orderly. And the flow of energy needs space and organization in order to more freely.

Clutter is a distraction—it affects your ability to concentrate, which means less productivity, frustration and less ability to enjoy life and business (which is not good for an entrepreneur!). There are six types of clutter; as you read this list, consider what is in your space right now because it could be sabotaging your business progress and results.

And yes—your home environment counts too… if your office is organized but your home is not, it can cause a sense of disconnect between who you are professionally and who you are personally. It can also distort your results. For example, you may bring money in through your business but find that you cannot hold on to it personally.

## The Six Types of Clutter

You may not realize all the forms that clutter can take… following is a list of the six major types of clutter that may be sabotaging your Feng Shui results without your knowledge.

1. **Everyday clutter:** anything that is unused, not loved, not needed, broken, messy, extra "stuff", a dust collector. The effect of it is your emotional stagnation, because it is stuck energy.

2. **Physical Body clutter:** anything that causes you to feel heavy, slow or bloated. The effect is that you don't have the "juice" to do what you need to do physically.

3. **Symbolic clutter:** anything that is a link to a negative memory, former relationship, promotes depression or a sinking feeling, something left undone. The effect of it is

your energy goes "down"; you might experience "beat 'em up" at yourself or wistful yearnings to something unhealthy or other emotions that don't pull you forward.

4. **"Past" clutter:** anything that is a "leftover" from a career, relationship or old way of being. The effect is that you aren't able to move forward cleanly, that you feel unresolved in some way with the break, or there's something left unsaid or undone to complete a situation, or that you don't trust the new way of being.

5. **Mind clutter:** anything that fills your brain to excess—to do lists, emails, information, TV, busywork. The effect is that you are not as effective as you could be, with no space for creativity and in a state of constant over-stimulation.

6. **E-clutter:** 'orphan' files on your computer, disorganized folders, over-flowing email, pictures that become distractions or even feel painful. The effect of it is that you can become distracted and overwhelmed when on your computer.

Where there is order and an open space that reflects who you are now, there can be positive energy flow. That is a generative force to create more of the results you want in your life and business.

# De-cluttering

A word about the de-cluttering process... many people find it's not that they want to hang on to stuff they don't want, appreciate or use anymore—it's that they don't know how to process the emotional attachment to the item to let go of it. Whatever the clutter item is can often be of sentimental value or some other perceived personal value to that person.

It's easy to get rid of stuff that has no meaning… but, if you remember the day you got it, or it is family memorabilia, or you think your kids might want it someday, it's tough to make the decision to let it go. When that comes up, explore those feelings, enjoy the memories, honor what the item brings up for you, and then decide again. If it's not an immediate answer, set it aside until you're ready to make the decision.

Remember if you can't say yes, it's a no. And, by the by, any time you say yes to one thing you are saying no to something else. If you decide you want to keep something, you are taking space for something new that could be coming in to you and, without having a place for it, you could be sending out an energetic message that signals you are not ready to receive your incoming abundance and, so, it will be blocked or diverted accordingly.

# Symbolism and Adjustments

*"The first step toward success is taken when you
refuse to be a captive of the environment
in which you first find yourself."*
~ Mark Caine

## Three Levels of Symbolism

Symbols have three levels of relevance. The level that is "furthest" from you is universal symbology; that is, universal symbols of wealth relate to all people anywhere. An example of a universal symbol of wealth is your stove because, in any culture anywhere in the world, if you have the ability to use the stove to cook nourishment, it indicates you have the means to buy/get food. Make sure your stove is in good working order, that all the burners work, and rotate using all the burners regularly. Some people tend to cook on just one burner out of four, which limits their ability to generate wealth energy to 25%.

The second layer of symbolic representation is cultural, which is something that has meaning for the country or culture in which you live. For people in the United States, the Liberty Bell would have special meaning, but people from other countries may not know or care about it.

And the third layer, which is the most significant because it is the closest to you, is comprised of the personal symbols that have meaning for you. Such objects might be the first dollar you ever earned, your childhood piggy bank, or a copy of your first paycheck. These objects hold meaning for you, but others would not relate to them the same way that you do. These symbols are actually the most powerful in activating your environment because you have an emotional connection to them.

## Three Levels of Adjustments

Now let's consider the three ways to influence, or adjust, your environment.

> First, you must consider the "mundane" in making changes to create more of what you want in your life. That is, it's pretty difficult to attract greater money when you live or work in a dirty, cramped, or dingy space. If you want to attract enhanced prosperity, you're going to have to work on the day-to-day, regular, mundane level to make it happen. We're talkin' good old-fashioned elbow grease and 'spiffy-ing up' what you have… OR moving to a new space!
>
> The second path to working with your environment is through adjustments. That is, through placing symbols and objects in certain areas, hanging crystals, and otherwise

redirecting energetic flow in your space, you can shift your relationship with your environment.

Lastly, the most direct but, potentially, the most difficult and the most powerful way to shift your environment is by working with transcendental energies through ritual, intention, and conscious connection. However, if the first two levels have been unaddressed, this method to create change is likely to be diminished in power, or possibly be ineffective, due to your demonstrated lack of willingness to work with the most basic energies.

## Adjusting Your Space

As humans, it is natural for us to filter out the familiar. It would be nearly impossible to drive down the street if our sensors weren't able to filter out the more ordinary aspects of driving. Starting a new job has a certain excitement and vitality because everything is new—six months into the job, things settle in because we are used to them. The same goes with our daily environments—we get used to them and it sometimes takes someone else with a fresh eye to help us see what we take for granted.

A great exercise is to take a tour of your space, paying particular attention to key items, décor and energy areas as we go to create an action plan for you to adjust to create more of what you want in your life and business. (Naturally, you will be ahead of the game if you "de-clutter" either as you go or before you get started.) In fact, take your camera with you to capture images of your space—you will be surprised (and maybe shocked) at what you can see in a picture you missed by merely looking at the environment yourself.

## Wealth Symbols

We entrepreneurs like money, so this section gives specific symbols and/or objects that "adjust" or work well to support your Wealth (see the Bagua Map section for more info).

**Water fountain:** be sure you can see both where the water is flowing from and the reservoir it is flowing in to in order to see your money moving and where it is being held.

**Waterfall picture:** of a beautiful place that resonates with you.

**Wind chime:** that ideally has eight rods made of metal or bamboo (eight being the number of big business and money).

**Prosperity Toad:** legend has it the toad visits only the homes of people who will receive money the next day. Note that once the I-Ching coin (ancient Chinese money) is placed in his mouth, it should not be removed or it will be unlucky.

**Plants:** lucky bamboo is the fastest growing, most resilient wood and also absorbs negativity. Jade plants have leaves shaped like coins. Rubber plants have large leaves to hold a lot of money. Ferns and dracaenas have downward motion to their leaves, like flowing water. Live plants are optimal, however, a good silk works really well if you don't have a "green thumb" (a silk plant is definitely better than a dead or dying real one).

**Frogs:** symbolize prosperity. Often you will see Oriental plant holders with a ring of frogs around the opening—that is to draw in abundance, especially when holding lucky bamboo wrapped in gold or red ribbon (which represents transformational energy).

# SYMBOLISM AND ADJUSTMENTS

**Aquarium:** should have nine fish to represent fulfillment, with one of them different (for example, eight goldfish and one black) to represent room the universal energies to bring you what it knows best. If you are dictating exactly what you want, you may be waiting a long time and/or the universe may want to bring you something better than you could have imagined but be restricted because of your "tight" request guidelines.

**Amethyst, Citrine or Turquoise:** these crystals vibrate to wealth energies and having them in your space supports the attraction of money.

**Personal symbols,** such as your dream home or desired vacation, work well in this area. Use the colors of purple, green and/or jewel tones to decorate in this area. Flowing water is flowing money—this area should feel "flow". However, if you decide you want to pump things up by showing rushing water (thinking that will make it come in faster), you could be creating a scenario where it goes so fast you either cannot tap into it or it is "dangerous" in some other way. That is, it comes in so quickly it comes from undesired sources, such as an inheritance, or too quickly to easily adapt to newfound wealth, such as winning the lottery.

## Other Adjustment Items

With new Feng Shui awareness, the next nine days are an optimal time to make as many adjustments as you can; following is a list of possible adjustments you could use in your space.

| Type of Energy | Specific Adjustments |
| --- | --- |
| Light Energy | Lights, mirrors, crystals, fire, reflective surfaces |
| Sound Energy | Bells, chimes, wind chimes, audio players, drums, musical instruments |
| Living Force, Vitality (includes Still Water) | Plants, flowers, aquariums, fishbowls, pets, still bird baths, swimming pools, colored water in a vase |
| Hydraulic Energy (Moving Water) | Fountains, waterfalls, streams, flowing birth baths, hot tubs, jacuzzi |
| Mobile Objects | Mobiles, windsocks, weathervanes, windmills, chimes, flags |
| Heavy Objects (Anchors) | Stones, statues, heavy furniture, trunks, weight set |
| Powered Objects | Appliances, computers, anything electronic |
| Color | All colors |
| Traditional Chinese Cure | Firecrackers, bamboo flutes, beaded curtains, foo dogs, coins |
| Fragrance | Essential oils, aromatherapy, incense, wood burning in fireplace, cooking, baking, candles |
| Other (Most Important) | Personal items of significance |

Remember working with your Feng Shui is a personal, dynamic process that has been used for thousands of years with success. You are where you are now as a result of your abilities to manifest. Shifts will occur; notice synchronicities, different ways of feeling, new opportunities. Your environment can support you in creating the life you want—listen to your intuition, make appropriate choices, take right action, pay attention and celebrate all your successes.

Another key point to adjusting your environment is to be aware of your intention in doing so; essentially, you are infusing your space with a new energy. Make sure you are clear on what you want, you have clear focus for your intention, that your intention is positive, active and in your best and highest good. By infusing your intention into your space through your adjustments, you are super-charging your results.

## Bagua Area Adjustments

In case you would like to activate a particular area of your Bagua, following is a listing of items appropriate for each area, depending on what outcome you want or what energy you want to invoke in your life or business.

### Career:

- Water fountain, waterfall, aquarium
- Pictures/posters of streams, oceans, lakes, waterfalls
- Career images & symbols
- Randomly shaped, free form objects
- Mirrors, glass, crystal
- Colors: black, dark colors, maroon, navy blue, chocolate brown, charcoal gray

### Knowledge and Self-Wisdom:

- Books, tapes, reference material
- Pictures of mountains, teachers, images in meditative contemplation
- Crystal ball or meditative ornaments or tools
- Beautiful mirror (to see yourself more clearly)
- Colors: deep blue, green

## Family:

- Healthy plants, any color of fresh cut flowers
- Posters, paintings or collages of ideal body images, family & friends,
- Plants and flowers, gardens & landscapes
- Wood for furniture & decorations
- Colors: blue, green

## Wealth and Prosperity:

- Wind chimes, windsocks, flags
- Valuable items, antiques, coins, crystals or pictures of these items
- Pictures & photos that represent the image and feeling of wealth
- Healthy plants with round, shiny leaves, may bloom in red, purple or blue
- Silk flowers in red, blue or purple
- Water feature—fountain or waterfall (for flow of prosperity), aquarium
- Colors: dark blues, purple, red

## Fame and Reputation:

- Diplomas, awards, prizes, acknowledgements
- Animal patterns or leather, feather, wool or bone display items
- Pictures/posters of animals, people, sunshine
- Colors: reds, orange, and yellow
- Shapes: triangular, conical, pyramid

## Love, Marriage and Communications:

- Pictures of love partner
- If desiring a marriage relationship, use pictures and images of couples together
- Hang or display matched pairs of things
- Decorate using two's of things (candles, pictures, throw blankets, etc.)
- Colors: red, pink, white

## Children & Creativity:

- Art by children
- Art/craft supplies, building material
- Toys, stuffed animals
- Circular, oval, arch-shaped items
- Metal

## Helpful People, Benefactors & Travel:

- Pictures of spiritual guides, gods, goddesses, angels
- Helpful people in your life (teachers, mentors, people who inspire or motivate you)
- Places to travel or traveled
- Personal association to spiritual, religious beliefs
- Special places
- Colors: white, black, gray

## Health:

- Healthy pictures
- Open space
- Colorful mobiles or windchimes
- Fresh flowers, herbs or light scent diffuser
- Bowl with decorative gravel and lucky bamboo
- Rectangular or square shapes (not too bulky or big though!)
- Colors: yellows, light earth tones, neutrals

# Entrepreneurial Essentials and Red Flags

*"Follow the grain in your own wood."*
~ Howard Thurman

Your environment can either nurture your life goals or create obstacles to overcome. Feng Shui is the key to balancing your life for the optimum chi flow. In other words, the cosmic breath of life will move freely and easily through your life as you align your environment to your goals. You don't have to believe in it, because it is what it is; however, by working with natural energies, you will get more of the results you want.

In the Feng Shui world, your environment mirrors who you really are and what you really think about yourself. And in the western work world, your office Feng Shui relates to your productivity, performance, recognition, attendance, reliability and workflow.

Following are some ideas of how your office environment translates to your unconscious self and could be supporting or sabotaging you.

| Condition | Result | Adjustment |
|---|---|---|
| Boxing yourself in | Creates limitations & desire to hide or protect yourself | Open your space to receive abundance without limitation |
| Mirror opposite your desk, reflecting your work | Increases your workload | Move, or remove, the mirror |
| Stacks of paper (vertical) | Feels like your work is endless with mountains of paper | Organize horizontally or in file cabinets. Rule of thumb: at least 50% of your desktop should be clearly seen daily. |
| "Active" floor filing system | Don't have a stable, clear foundation from which to grow; putting obstacles that need to be climbed in your path | Clear your floor space for a solid and spacious foundation to support your goal achievement |
| Trash can is dominant (first thing you see) | Nothing you do is good enogh or worth your energy | Move to a less obvious place or position a plant near it |
| Small, cramped work area (clutter cramping your actual desk work area); low ceiling | Feeling of confinement and not being able to get everything done; stifled in reaching for your dreams; no room to grow | Clear, sort, file clutter to create room for expansion, arrange space to have |
| Back is to the door when seated at desk | Vulnerable to surprise or attack, drains your energy and creates unease | Rearrange your chair to be in the command position or place mirror to see what's coming in behind you |

# ENTREPRENEURIAL ESSENTIALS AND RED FLAGS

A clear desk means your work is flowing. Remember, you can also activate the Bagua of your desk! As you learned, the Bagua Map shows how energy flows and corresponds to each of the nine areas of your life. Simply turn the Bagua Map so the bottom of it (self-wisdom, career and helpful people) is aligned with your chair as you sit at your desk. The mouth of chi of your desk is where you sit to generate and handle your business.

That means to use the map, you want to align the bottom of the map with your chair—the farthest left hand corner diagonally from you when sitting is your wealth (abundance, opportunity, money, promotions, raises, bonuses), farthest across in the middle is fame and reputation (credit and recognition you receive for your work, what people are saying about you), and the farthest right-hand corner diagonally is relationships (with your colleagues, your boss and your clients).

It is ideal to make goals and determine which one or two you are going to focus on right now. Then activate the appropriate area on your desk and in your space for results. (Remember the Bagua may orient differently for your office vs. your desk, based on the mouth of chi—the door or your chair.) You can see the items listed in the Adjustments section to not which will have similar effects in your office or on your desk.

A note on adjustment items: remember the items that have personal meaning for you will have the most power in adjusting your space. If you don't see an item listed here, but it feels right, go ahead and use it. Your inner guidance supersedes anything that is generally recommended.

## Red Flags

It is important to note and correct any chi "shredders" in your space, such as nails or hooks protruding from walls that are unused, light fixtures or windows that are broken or cracked walls. Windows represent your vision, and walls represent security and safety. If either is compromised in your Wealth area, for example, you could be experiencing a lack of vision or security around your money. Make sure that mirrors are clean, not cracked and that the silver backing is whole, or you could be experiencing fragmented or tired money energy. Determine whether things need to be repaired or replaced. For example, if you don't use that floor lamp anyway, get rid of it. (Someone else somewhere needs it.)

The other point about your Wealth area is that you most easily attract abundance when you are in alignment with your life's purpose. If you are in a job where you find it difficult to get up in the morning, "hate" going to work, find yourself playing hooky to get out of going to work or cranky on a daily basis after working, these are signs that you are not in the right place to attract money. If this is your situation, look at what attracted you to the position in the first place, note what has changed (if anything, and generally it's you), and what you really want to be doing. Remember, any blockages in this area of your space represent obstacles in your ability to attract money.

The position of your desk is a really critical piece of Feng Shui placement that could have a major impact on your business. You want to make sure it's in the "Command Position", which means it is not directly in front of the door (but diagonal to it), that your back is supported, and that you are facing or can see the door.

Consider the view from your desk—it should pull you forward, since that is what is affecting you. Consider what is behind you, as that is the energy being absorbed into your energy body (if you have a picture of a cute hobo hanging behind your desk, where you sit and create money, it's likely that you feel like you could join the hobo!).

Make sure there are no sharp corners pointing at you (that will cut your personal chi, especially if you sit with the corner of two walls pointing at you). And if you find yourself boxed in when sitting at your desk, you are creating limitations for yourself. (Of course, if your "floor filing system" is activated, that is you putting mountains to climb smack-dab in the middle of your path!)

## Other Big Red Flags

Notice if you have any of the following in your environment; if you do, consider it a '911' for your attention!

- A mirror that reflects the work you have to do back to you (it doubles your work energetically)
- Your "to do" list is in your Wealth area on your desk or in your office (so you have plenty of work to do always); same goes for oversized in-boxes.
- Uncomfortable furniture that doesn't allow your body to relax for creative flow.
- Poor lighting which keeps your business in the dark.
- Your trash can or paper shredder being the first thing you see when you walk in the door (sets the tone for you—energy goes right in the garbage).
- Dark corners that collect stagnant energy and become energy suckers.
- Broken "stuff" that signals unfinished business, lack of time, apathy or scarcity to fix or replace it.

- Art that symbolizes or represents anything that is negative, toxic or dark.
- Too many emails sitting in your virtual inbox; this is a virtual energy drain and e-clutter.
- No plants, which are a symbol of living chi (even a good silk is better than nothing!).
- No natural light from windows—use full-spectrum bulbs to compensate.
- Old / former client files stacked up, taking space that could be for new clients.
- Anything else you are "tolerating" in your space (a squeaky door, a propped up table leg, an old sign on your door that doesn't have your name/title on it, etc.) or that "distracts" your energy (odd noises, things that feel out of place, etc.).

You can use aromatherapy, color, music, being organized, or air quality machines to help offset some of the above red flags. You may also want to consider how much "emf" (electro-magnetic force) energy is in your space; that is, if you have a lot of power lines or electricity that will, especially in a small space, have a negative effect on your energy.

One last note: know that Feng Shui isn't magic. It won't take the place of everyday action to achieve your goals. It does harness the power of your environment to work for you, and it transcends the "rational" in doing so, but you are the most important part of your environment.

# Activating Your Environment

*"People do not attract that which they want,
but that which they are."*
~ James Allen, *As A Man Thinketh*

The process of activating your environment occurs through all of what has been discussed so far: knowing your intention, making adjustments, using symbolism, working with specific areas of your Bagua, and paying attention to the first impression you have in your space (that often will give you the best information).

## Clarity of Intention

With any venture into the future, meaning a statement of what is desired, it is important to be clear on your focus and intention of what is being created. This is emphasized to an even greater degree when you are using Feng Shui, or any manifesting tools, in your life. You are connecting directly with the energy and the power of your surroundings, so it is vital you be clear and aware of what you are creating.

When you partner with your environment, you add synergy to your manifestation process, practically magnetizing the attraction mechanism of your "outer body" (your environment). You are creating extra momentum and, when your goals are in focus and your life is in harmony, you optimize the speed at which the manifestation process can occur. You WILL create powerful new results for yourself! Know what you are asking for—and then be open to receiving it!

# Your Feng Shui Action Plan

Knowing what you know now, what three intentions do you have for your life and business?

## Primary Objectives:

1. _____
2. _____
3. _____

You now have enough information to be able to determine how to adjust to create that new energy. Note below up to nine adjustments you can make for positive new results. (Nine being the universal number of completion.)

## Primary Adjustments:

1. _____
2. _____
3. _____
4. _____
5. _____
6. _____
7. _____
8. _____
9. _____

## Managing Expectations

How do you know when your chi is stuck? When you are not getting the results you want. How do you know what will happen when you start working with your Feng Shui to shift your relationship with your environment? You don't. However, that doesn't mean don't do it—that's like asking for a divorce before you've even met your mate!

Working through change, especially when it comes to money, is not easy. Period. Your Feng Shui reflects your core beliefs about yourself, your business, your value, and your trust in the world you know. Making shifts around your life and business can be easier with a positive attitude, to be sure. However, people naturally resist change as they gravitate toward something called "homeostasis", or stability. People don't really like to be changed, as a general rule—it's much better to change voluntarily and proactively.

You need to know you will probably experience resistance, or obstacles, at some level, and these moments are really learning opportunities from which to grow most significantly. Issues are disguised opportunities to learn and change for something better. And your higher self will protect you through "speed bumps" that cause you to stop, look and listen. Many people decide to not do what it takes to grow in their relationship with money, as evidenced by the economic status of the majority of our general society.

If you've ever had a massage where the therapist was working on your back, and your leg started to hurt, you've experienced what is called "referred pain". Sometimes you will experience that in your life as well. It might be the case where you are working on generating money when you realize you aren't in the right business, or making the right connections, or continue to make the wrong buying decisions. Referral pain lets you know that you need to address the core of your issue, not just the symptoms.

In working to create change in your business energy, you may find other areas of your life are greatly affected in unexpected ways—like dominoes all toppling when the first one knocks over the next one and then the next. Deciding to create change in your relationship with money is likely to create change in many other areas of your life. Proceed at the pace that is comfortable for you. If you are moving at a pace that feels uncomfortable or is unleashing a lot of unexpected outcomes, you have the option to slow down. You have your whole life to live yet…and only you can live it, so it's not going anywhere without you. (At the same time, anyone who knows me knows that for me, personally, change happens at an accelerated rate! And that's ok too… whatever works for you to live your best life is best.)

In working with clients, it's often the emotional attachment to the way things were or are that causes the biggest reluctance to change.

Fear of the unknown is scary—attachment to what was is at least familiar, even if dysfunctional. By working through those emotions and letting go of the known, you will shift to new places and receive new energy—in this case, new business opportunities and revenue potential.

# In Closing

*"The universe is just the way we think it is —
and that's why."*
~ John Woods

There is a lot that goes into attracting, creating and having business results intentionally, including being ready and being open to receiving the opportunities and money messages. Be willing to experience all that comes as a result of working with your personal Feng Shui; after all, one cannot receive with closed arms.

Please remember you create your conditions for your success. When you have removed the obstacles and positioned yourself as an attractor for success (in whatever goal you pursue), it occurs.

*You're living the results of your
Feng Shui every day.*

*Why not do it consciously —
for the business results
you intentionally desire?*

# Appendices

# The Top Ten Ways That Feng Shui Supports You

Feng Shui, which literally means "wind" and "water", is the art and science of infusing intention into your environment—or external body—to create maximum support to help you achieve your goals and the life you want to create. When your external body (or your physical surroundings) is out of alignment, it drains your energy and makes it harder to get where you want to go.

Feng Shui has restorative powers, for when you feel good in your environment, chances are that you are ready for just about anything. This is the difference between Feng Shui that does and doesn't support you as you live your life. Feng Shui is a tool you can use to help you get to where you want to be in your life. We live Feng Shui every day—why not get do it consciously and get the results you want?

1. **Working with Feng Shui to consciously enhance your environment is the fastest way to change your life—right now.**

    The top three determinants of life path are 1) fate, 2) luck, 3) environment, 4) philanthropy and 5) education and experience. Note what comes in last, and that the first two are not really influence-able by anybody. The first powerful level that we really have access to in our lives to influence our future is working with the environment.

2. **Feng Shui works with chi flow.**

   Chi flow, literally "cosmic breath", is the way your space breathes, the way your body breathes, and the way you breathe in your space. If you're not breathing, you're not living.

3. **Energy exchange is a basic principle of life.**

   There is an energy exchange between our bodies and the vibrations of energy in our surroundings—our external body. This energetic exchange can either inspire us or totally overwhelm us.

   For example, if you are not comfortable in your office, it's likely that you will not want to spend time there (much less a major part of your day), or feel that there isn't enough time to get everything done, or that things are unstable or that you're exhausted when you got home. In the long view, this means that you could be losing money because the energetic exchange between you and your environment is not supportive for you to operate at maximum capability.

   We have all experienced this principle on some level; for example, when you have worked really hard to close the end of the year in your business, run all the errands for the holiday, made sure your home is ready for company, spend time with friends for weeks on end... only to get sick on the holiday? That is Feng Shui—the universe is compensating for the big energy push with making sure you slow down and get some rest.

4. **Paying attention to the details that comprise your life (i.e., your environment) is often the first step toward getting where you want to go.**

   By taking into account where you are in your life right now, where you want to go and/or be in your life, the timing of your choice to change (ideally, right now), and your physical surroundings, Feng Shui helps you to assess your options, provide a framework for action and create the conscious change you want in your life.

5. **Changing your life is as easy as changing your environment.**

   All it takes is letting your environment know your intentions (your goals) and working with natural energies to get good chi flow.

   In other words, what your environment looks and feels like is a reflection of what you think about your life. The energy exchange between you and your environment can help you realize your goals and desires or cause them to get lost in translation. By placing elements, colors and shapes in lucky, or "auspicious", positions in our environment, you can influence your wealth, relationships, health, careers or any area of your life to change in the direction you really want in life.

6. **When your environment, such as workspace, is clear, you feel free, creative and motivated.**

   Why? Because there is room to create, the universe has space to bring you the resources you desire to get what you want, and because you don't have to overcome physical clutter and emotional reaction to it in order to be productive.

7. **Working with the power of Feng Shui principles inherently means looking at your space / life with new eyes.**

   Looking at your environment with the eyes of a stranger means seeing details that we take for granted every day. Often, we overlook what is right in front of us. New perspective creates many opportunities, including those from already existing resources or from having space to generate new avenues. It becomes our choice as to what we want to pursue.

8. **Feng Shui is about object placement, symbolism and personal intention in your physical environment.**

   While some may consider Feng Shui to be interior decorating on its' most superficial level, the degree of intention, awareness and conscious commitment are the keys to good personal Feng Shui. What works for your colleague may not work for you, and vice-versa; it's all relative to what's happening with you at this time in your space with where you want to go. In fact, when working with a practitioner, you should not disclose personal rituals, cures or adjustments, as the effects of the solution may become diluted.

9. **By applying the principles of Feng Shui, consideration is given to efficiency, organization and visual orientation.**

   In order for your environment to support you, you must feel organized, with items you need in proper reaching distances, with colors attuned to you and appropriate chi flow. Your efficiency will be enhanced because you will know exactly where to find what you need exactly when you need it. Add aesthetic appeal, and you will have a visually pleasing system that works well for (and with) you.

# THE TOP TEN WAYS THAT FENG SHUI SUPPORTS YOU

10. **Feng Shui doesn't have memory.**

    Feng Shui doesn't really care how you got to where you are, so the fact that you have always had a big junk drawer isn't important. Rather, it is observing that the big junk drawer lacks organization, could be weighing you down or clogging some aspect of your life or business, or might represent unnecessary baggage in some area. It tends to be both forgiving, in not being judgmental or remembering the error of your past ways, but also unforgiving, in that it is very literal. Be careful what you ask for, as it is likely you will get it.

Your observations and gut reaction will tell you where to start with your personal Feng Shui. By re-designing your environment, you can shift the exchange of energy and get your chi moving to create the life you want. Feng Shui can help you make and create the changes you want in your life—right now.

# The Feng Shui of Logos

In the world of Feng Shui, everything is Feng Shui. That is, everything we see, read, think, respond to, are stimulated by, take in and more relates to the symbols that we create or have in our lives.

In business, one of the most important symbols is the company logo. This is the most visible symbol of the company's self-image; it is the public face that people see and identify with in the marketplace. For example, when you see a red bullseye, what company do you think of immediately?

The logo "tangibilizes" the company's image for the public and has a significant effect on how the public perceives the company. Often people see the logo first, as we think in symbols, before reading the name or anything else about the company. Everything in life is represented by symbols. It is vital that you choose or create the appropriate symbols for your business logo, as that will have a clear impact on your success or lack of it.

One company example of a negative logo is the Enron symbol—a square cube balanced precariously on one of its sharp edges, just ready to fall over. Which is what the company eventually did. Microsoft has a wavy square "flag" with four colored squares inside it—when the left edge is open, it suggests being open to receiving everything without discernment, including viruses. If Microsoft were to close the square, they would create a protected system, and would minimize potential input of threats to their products.

Consider placement of the company's signage; the higher it is, the higher the heights that your business may attain. If your sign is too low, while it indicates being grounded, the business may never really take off. Something anchored securely (as opposed to blowing in the wind like with awnings, flags or balloons) is preferred to suggest permanence.

If your address includes lucky numbers, such as 1, 6, 7, 8 or 9, be sure to emphasize them. Be sure that your address clearly shows from the street at night in the dark.

Be sure to match the color of your logo to your business. A medical office would do well to use yellow or green for health and life force energy. A creative enterprise, like advertising, would benefit by lots of white in their logo representing creativity.

It is important that your logo is clear and easy to understand. A cluttered logo that is too clever causes confusion and loses the audience, which repels success.

# Top Ten Reasons to Feng Shui Both Your Home and Office

1. **Both aspects of your external body deserve your time and attention.**

   It is your body and it's worth attending to in a consistent, caring and genuine way. Would you do less for your pet? Your physical body? Your child? If you answered that you would do more for anyone else but yourself, it's a big indicator of an issue that needs some attention.

2. **Consistency—attention to one environment and not the other means unequal energy distribution.**

   The laws of nature state that there must be equal energy distribution, so the balance will necessarily happen somewhere else. For example, you'll want to hang out in a great little coffee shop or find yourself at a friend's home instead of at your own home, or you'll find reasons to be out of your office to avoid your workspace.

3. **The time you spend in each space comprises probably 80–90% of your time daily; it is important to feel connected to and with each environment.**

   Good Feng Shui in both helps to balance spending too much time in either space. Conversely, if not addressed and balanced, the one that is unbalanced through Feng Shui could result in your disconnection with the space. This means you won't want to spend time there or find life situations a little more difficult to handle in some way.

4. **The universe will bring to you what you ask with intention and focus—especially if it is asked in a consistent, clear manner.**

   Setting your intentions in one environment and not the other is a mixed message. The universe will try to decipher what you are trying to say, and it's very literal. For example, if at home you focus on activating and progressing your current career, but you don't pay attention to what's happening in your workspace, you could experience misunderstandings with your superiors or colleagues, be passed over for the very promotion you seek, or find yourself on the outside of the power base.

5. **Essentially, the result of not fully committing to balance and nurture yourself / your external body is self-sabotage.**

   You are the only one responsible for taking care of your needs and wants. Knowing the transformational and restorative powers that Feng Shui brings to your environment, and not harnessing that power to bring you to your highest self is only hurting you and keeping you from your highest potential.

6. **Each environment potentially has multiple personalities/variables attached; each environment has to balance accordingly.**

   Different people and different situations will impact you differently, and your environment may need to support you differently for overall balance. For example, in the office, you may need to keep stress levels down, and need lots of calming, de-stressing elements, whereas at home, you want to feel energized and revitalized with lots of yang elements.

7. **The application of Feng Shui principles in both your home and work environments ensures your maximum progress toward your goals.**

   Balancing one environment without the other is like leaving a project half done, and you will potentially feel incomplete or uncomfortable in the unbalanced space. That will translate to you feeling like you don't want to be there, and you may become inundated with minutiae that keeps you busy or distracted from true productivity, or your calendar may book up with engagements or meetings unnecessarily.

8. **Like the layers of an onion, each area that you activate in each environment will produce results and potentially other issues to address.**

   Working with one environment may reveal issues or challenges in the other. For example, you may adjust your relationships area at work and find that you are arguing with family or roommates at home or friends outside of work. This is actually a gift from the universe, because it is showing you where you need to spend some immediate time and focus.

Conversely, if you experience resistance to making changes, this could be an indicator of some sort of energetic drain (an attachment to an outcome, an unfulfilled need, fear, etc.).

9. **There are really several environments within your home and workspaces that need to be addressed for the most holistic approach.**

   According to Thomas Leonard, considered the 'grandfather' of the coaching industry, these environments are: physical space (home, office), nature (or out of doors) environment, memetic environments (ideas, thoughts), emotional environments (feelings, states), energy environments (electrical, nutritional, etc.), people environments (friends, family, colleagues) and time environments (time of day, how you spend your time). Imagine a world where all your environments are in balance… you will no longer need to tolerate distractions, being uncomfortable, stress, misunderstandings, unhappiness, unrest, ill health, financial or emotional drains… what an achievable aspiration!

10. **Energy is linked to you from either place as you move through your day; an energy drain in either will be felt in the other environment.**

    If you feel unsupported in your home space, work is likely to be more difficult. If your workday or workflow is difficult, then it is likely that relaxing at home takes longer or it is more difficult to enjoy your personal life. The goal is to be able to be productive and happy in order to enjoy a balanced, robust and fulfilling life—whatever that means for you.

# Feng Shui Frequently Asked Questions

## What is Feng Shui?

Pronounced *fung shway*, the words literally mean "wind" and "water" in Chinese. This ancient Chinese art focuses on balancing surroundings with the people who live or work in a space. Contrary to what some people think, Feng Shui is not a religion—it is a practice of conscious alignment between the inner and outer worlds. In Feng Shui, your environment is your "external body"; you interact or exchange energy with it and, as a result, experience either harmony or disarray. Literally, your environment helps or hurts you in manifesting your life goals and desires.

## Feng Shui seems like a fad. How does it work?

Feng Shui actually goes back about 4,000 years, when the Chinese wanted to find the best final resting place for their relatives in order to ensure the best lives for the descendants still living and in future generations. Feng Shui was introduced to the Western world about 20 years ago, so it probably seems new. It works by object placement and symbolism, aligning elements and items in your environment in patterns to cause your surroundings to support and enhance your career, relationships, prosperity or any area of life in which you desire change. It actualizes your true intention.

## Isn't Feng Shui just fancy interior design?

While some people choose to think of it as a superficial modification of homes and offices, it actually produces results by working on several levels. Not only is the physical level affected, but the emotional, intellectual and metaphysical levels of being become energized to support your life. Object placement and symbolism are important; however, intention and clarity of purpose are just as important, if not more so.

The top five determinants of life path are 1) fate, 2) luck, 3) environment, 4) philanthropy and 5) education and experience. Note what comes in last, and that the first two are not really influence-able by anybody. The first powerful level that we really have access to in our lives to enhance our lives and our future is working with the environment.

## What's involved in a Feng Shui consultation?

Each practitioner has their own set of techniques, skills and rituals that work with their energy, and each practitioner may do a consultation differently. There may be a phone call or exchange of information to zero in on the issues at hand. There may also be preparation that the client can do to maximize the time together in the consultation. The practitioner might conduct a pre-consult intention meditation, and then work with the client in the space (home or office).

During the consultation, the client may take notes or the practitioner can write up a report on the findings and recommendations. There are times during a consultation that it is appropriate for the practitioner to perform transcendental rituals, as well as inform about mundane cures and major adjustments.

After the consultation, the practitioner typically does a closing meditation to support the client in their desires. If the client has clarifying questions about anything that came up during the consultation, the practitioner is commonly available for answers by phone or email.

## Is it ok for my friends / family to be there during my consultation?

You are the person bringing the Feng Shui practitioner into your space, so you are the decision-maker as to who you'd like to have there. It can be really helpful to have the people who share the space with you present.

However, there are a couple of considerations in making that decision. Feng Shui is powerful because it works with you (and, by association, anyone else inhabiting the space), in your environment, at that moment in time, with your specific goals—that can get really personal. Feng Shui is also all about energy—having additional energy present will have an effect on the consultation.

## Can I tell my friends what works for me so it will work for them too?

While there are some basics that apply to everyone in Feng Shui, it is often tailored exactly to your needs, in your environment, at this moment, with your goals. What works for you may not produce the same results for your friend / family—it is actually with caution that you should share what happened in your consultation. The more that you share the specifics, the more the energy dilutes (or the less energy you have to shift things in your life).

## What if I like my stuff right where it is?

There are a couple of things to think about here. If your life is feeling "stuck" and everything is where it has been for a while, there may be a causal relationship. The old adage "Do everything the same way and expect different results is the definition of insanity" applies to this situation. And the goal of Feng Shui is not to disrupt your entire life in a chaotic way, but rather, to bring balance. You can always try a new placement of things, be aware of changes that result, and move it back if you don't like what's happening.

By being aware of where you want to go and/or be in your life, the timing of your choice to change (ideally, right now), and your physical surroundings, Feng Shui helps you assess your options, provide a framework for action and create the conscious change you want.

## Will I just have to move and start all over again?

Sometimes it feels like it! But no… it's not very often that a Feng Shui practitioner encourages that sort of drastic action. Just about everything in Feng Shui is relative—that means it can be adjusted to be more auspicious (beneficial) to you. Feng Shui is about flow, which means flexibility and adaptation.

## What happens if I don't do what is recommended during the consultation?

Of course, the choice is up to you. However, once you learn something, you cannot unlearn it. If you knowingly do not follow through on something that will be beneficial to you, you have made a decision to move another direction and will get different results. It is important to understand why the recommendations were made to you, so that you can reinforce the positive benefits of your actions. If you don't understand or appreciate the recommendation, ask to learn if there might be another way to accomplish the same results—at the very least, learn why the recommendation was made so you can assist in creating a solution that works for you.

# Glossary of Feng Shui Terms

*"What you are, so is your world. Everything in the universe is resolved into your own inward experience. It matters little what is without, for it is all a reflection of your own state of consciousness. It matters everything what you are within, for everything without will be mirrored and colored accordingly."*
~ Path to Prosperity

It is important to create a common language as you discover how to best work with your environment to achieve your business goals. Following are some basic definitions and foundational concepts to the material that will be presented throughout this course.

**Feng Shui:** is the ancient Chinese art and science of infusing conscious intention into your environments and working with natural energies to achieve your goals. Every culture has a similar belief system that works with natural energy flow, but Feng Shui has gotten a lot of press recently which has popularized this masterful Chinese system into "fad" status.

The words "feng" and "shui" literally mean "wind" and "water", which are the only two things we humans cannot live without (well, for very long anyway!). The main objective of Feng Shui is for you to be in harmony with your life and goals at this time in your life and in your current environment(s). That is, there are four elements to positive and supportive personal Feng Shui: you, your goals, your environment, at this time. There are many schools of Feng Shui; this program is based on the tools and techniques of the Black Sect of Tantric Buddhism school (commonly known as "Black Hat" Feng Shui) as founded by Grand Master Lin Yun.

**Environments:** are literally your external, outer or "other", bodies. Environments surround us, nurture and protect us, and reflect back to us our manifestation of our beliefs. While that may sound confusing, it's really pretty basic. Everything around you is an environment. So, as examples, your physical environment is your external body, your friends and loved ones are your social body, your career is your money-generating body, and your thought environment is what creates ALL your environments. The physical space strategies contained in this course pertain to both your home and office environments. There are also some tips on how to work with your innermost environments to shift your internal relationship with money.

**Chi:** is a Chinese word that has no direct translation into English. The closest we come to an accurate translation is "breath of life". Every person or thing has chi, which is life force energy—including inanimate objects. Chi, and chi flow, is a basic measure of how an environment is either positively or negatively affecting us. When chi is missing or negative, we feel sluggish, stuck or even fearful. When chi is positive and/or flowing, we are happy, energized and optimistic. When in an environment, consider how a river would flow through the space from the main doorway to get an idea of

# GLOSSARY OF FENG SHUI TERMS

the chi flow of that space. Notice where it stops, winds around and leaves the space to understand how to work with the chi of that particular room.

**Clutter:** is anything that you no longer love and/or no longer serves you. If it's something you can live without, chances are you should and someone else can use it. Clutter is also anything that gives you a negative emotional charge—the picture of your ex, the memento from the worst vacation ever, the bank statements left over from your starving student days, etc. Clutter is the number one chi blocker! We'll be talking about how to determine if your money chi is stuck.

**Activate:** means to unleash the potential energy of the area or object in order for it to support you in attaining your goals. For example, if there is stuck or stagnant energy in the Feng Shui area that pertains to your Wealth, it is important to activate that energy to get your money moving. There are three levels to activation: the mundane, through making adjustments and through transcendental processes working directly with universal energies. This course touches on all three levels of activation.

**Adjustments:** changes you make to your environment on the physical or energetic level by using items of symbolism, intention and/or ritual.

**Manifestation:** is the actualization of your wants, needs and desires. It's a big word that says you create our experiences through aligning the vibration of your thoughts, choices and action. You are responsible for everything in your life that now exists. If you don't like what you have or where you are, it's time to make some new manifestation decisions!

# Feng Shui Self-Quiz

1. What does Feng Shui mean literally?

List four principles of chi.

2. _____
3. _____
4. _____
5. _____
6. What is the Theory of Relativity? _____
   _____

7/8/9. The three layers of symbolism are: _____, _____, _____.

10/11/12. The three layers of adjustments are: _____, _____, _____.

13/14. What are two of the five environments that affect everyone's life from a cosmic perspective?
_____, _____.

Name three good Feng Shui enhancers in any environment.

15. _____

16. _____

17. _____

18. What is the Feng Shui energy map of any environment called?

19. What is the purpose of the "reinforcement of the three secrets"?

20. In an office environment, what is the most important thing to consider?

If you answered at least 16 of these questions correctly, congratulations—you have done a great job of understanding Feng Shui!

# Bonus

As a gift for working with your Feng Shui, please download a copy of my ebook called *Evolving Your Environment: 177 Ways To Create The Conditions For Success*.

Summary: A 35-page ebook chock-full of tips, insights and practical how-to's to literally program your environment to get what you want in life.

Environments are our mirrors. What we see around is a result of decisions that we've made in the past, which were based on our thoughts at the time and with the resources we had in that moment. These environments may or may not reflect who we are now and may or may not pull us forward into our success.

In order to get different results, it is important to "program" our environments differently. Our environments contain the power and the energy to help us attain our goals. For example, if a bedroom is decorated in bright, bold, "loud" colors, it isn't likely to help us attain our goal of getting solid rest. If we tone down the colors (without even addressing other possible changes!), it is likely that we will sleep more restfully.

Being aware of the energy in our environments is the first step to positive transformation. After all, if we don't know what is happening where we are, it is more difficult to *change* where we are to get a different result. Understanding what is NOW helps us to consciously create our FUTURE. This ebook gives you a way to start creating more of what you want in very practical ways.

Just go to this page to get your complimentary copy of this ebook now!

**FlowingFengShui.com/Harmony**

# About the Author

**LYNN SCHEURELL**
Feng Shui Master | Clarity Teacher
Business Catalyst and Advisor

Lynn Scheurell, writer, teacher and professional catalyst, is an authority on translating nebulous and/or complex concepts to clear, concise language that effectively communicates life-changing ideas.

Since 1998, she has worked with more than 7,000 people to discover their unique essence to deliver it through their businesses, books and presentations. Feng Shui is her original modality and remains a core of her work.

By definition, a catalyst provokes significant change; this is what people expect in working with Lynn. She is an innovator and facilitator of the complex made simple. Concurrently, Lynn also knows the proven keys to business success in systems, marketing and strategic action.

She has had serial entrepreneurial ventures (online *and* brick and mortar) since her teens in such diverse businesses as: a specialty boutique retail shop, a resume writing business, a home staging business, working as a professional intuitive, personal / entrepreneurial development mentor and writer.

All these opportunities, as well as consistent continuing education through workshops, seminars, classes, group training and private mentoring (both as mentee and mentor), developed her innovation and brainstorming skills, lateral systems thinking capabilities and high sensitivity to unseen energies that can be utilized to optimize flow and intentional results.

Her formal education was received through the University of Wisconsin–Milwaukee, graduating with a B.S. in Criminal Justice.

Focusing on writing several books and sharing magic with wonderful clients, Lynn currently resides near Palm Springs, CA. She considers herself to be a practical visionary, idea generator and facilitator of positive transformation through sharing compelling clarity.

See **FlowingFengShui.com** and **LynnScheurell.com** for more info.

# More of what people are saying about Lynn Scheurell:

"I had my apartment re-aligned with a Feng Shui practitioner, Lynn Scheurell. Lynn is amazing and does many, many types of consultations to help you get the most energy from your workspace or home. Her talent and intuition is inherent and she is a phenomenal and gifted Feng Shui practitioner who can truly make your environment more balanced and productive."

~ Rhonda Renee O'Neil, Manager

"In working with Lynn, she continues to act in the presence of an emerging reality that clearly reflects my hopes and dreams. Her skills transform the whole system rather than putting band-aid on one part of the whole! I have evolved and find myself utilizing new ways and means, which are uplifting. Lynn inspires success! Lynn lives in field of being where all answers exist!"

~ Patricia Deck, Entrepreneur

"Thank you so much for the "Feng Shui For Lovers" class. I have heard a variety of stories from friends the power of Feng Shui but never really embraced the ideal for my own home. I thought the power within me was enough to change everything around me.

As you stated in the class Feng Shui facilitates the flow of power so all aspects within the home and in your life come easier. As you explained the principals of Feng Shui, it all made such common sense. I began using the simple principals that you suggested on my home and it immediately felt more relaxing and integrated. I even got a date with someone I really liked within a few days and hope to see her again. The proof for me is in how I feel more productive and comfortable than I ever have before in my home. Thanks."

~ Bart Sharp, Intuitive Healer

"My partner, Bob, and I hired Lynn to Feng Shui our home. We love our Palm Springs home but neither of us was sleeping well here, and there was just a sense that there was a flow problem in the house. Bob is an interior designer so we were concerned that Feng Shui would disrupt the design aspect of the house.

Lynn was terrific. She surveyed the house from front to back and explained problem areas in a way that made real sense to two novices in the art of Feng Shui. Her recommendations did not interfere with any interior design aspects and in fact Bob was able to create new features that complement the design as well as fulfill the chi flow of the home.

Lynn was able to nail the chi problem in the bedroom that was preventing our restful sleep. An attached master bath was pulling our chi down the open toilet. Up lighting and a water feature in our living room resulted an almost immediate release in money issues and provided some much needed flow in that area.

One recommendation nearly backfired on us but proved that Feng Shui works. We put a box under our bed with certain objects in it to precipitate better chi. Unfortunately we didn't realize that the box had a mirrored top that reflected the chi back on itself. Once corrected, things changed dramatically and we began getting a restful sleep.

Lynn has made believers out of us and we would highly recommend her services to anyone looking to improve their lives through Feng Shui."

~ Lee North, Astrologer


"Lynn is the epitomy of "feel, good, safe energy"~~ no matter if she's doing feng shui, astrology, numerology or just a reading this woman makes you feel good and provides clean clarity!. She has powerful, positive insight and is completely right on. She's loving, kind and without judgement – awesome!!!!!!!"

~ Genz Z, Real Estate Broker

## Other Books from Lynn Scheurell:

7 Mistakes That Keep World-Changing Business Owners From Making Money: (And How To Avoid Them!)

Defining Your Prosperity Path: How to Make Opportunities (And A Living!) From Your Wisdom

Going From Good To Guru: 10 Crucial Things You Can Do To Help More People And Grow Your Business Faster And Easier

How To Make Friends With Your Money As An Entrepreneur: A Money Friendship Self-Quiz And Action Plan

Own The Wisdom Within: 5 Keys to Using Life's Turning Points for Transformational Success

The Bigger Message: Understanding Universal Context to Live Your Best Life Now Through Conscious Awareness

The Energy of Money: Understanding Your Money Messages: Discover How the Universe is Talking to You

The Entrepreneurial Guidebook: How To Reach Your Potential, Help More People And Change The World

The Rituals of Creating Money: Ways to Play to Get More of What You Want

You've Arrived!: A 5-Step System to Bypass Your Logical Mind, Activate Your Intuitive Potential and Gain Perfect Clarity For Your Business

www.ingramcontent.com/pod-product-compliance
Lightning Source LLC
Chambersburg PA
CBHW072059290426
44110CB00014B/1748